Sincere Advice to Those Who Fell Away from Islam

a reasonable discussion with those who are deluded by Western culture

'Abd al-Raḥmān bin Nāṣir al-Sa'dī

(died 1376 h.) رَحِمَهُ ٱللَّهُ

This book is dedicated to all those who have been misled by this world and Shayṭān as a kind invitation back to Islam. Do not despair of Allah's Mercy.

'Abd al-Raḥmān al-Sa'dī

مَكْتَبَةُ الثَّقَافِي

THAQAFA PRESS

CONTENTS

Author's Introduction[1]

The following is an account of a discussion between two men who were both once Muslim and associates. They both used to practice the same faith and had once busied themselves with seeking religious knowledge. They were separated for a lengthy period and then reunited.

Surprisingly, the state of the one who had been abroad transformed, and his character had changed. So his colleague questioned him, only to find to his surprise that he had been overtaken by atheistic propaganda that promotes abandoning religion and rejecting what the Messengers brought.

His associate proceeded to make a heartfelt attempt to turn him away from such a strange transformation but was unsuccessful in his effort. Subsequently, he realized that this was a tremendous ailment and sickness, requiring him to uproot the disease and treat it with the most effective of cures. He realized that this was dependent upon

---

[1] This advice was initially written by the author as a series of newspaper articles. Later they were combined and published as a treatise under the title *Intiṣār al Ḥaqq* (The Triumph of Truth).

understanding the factors causing him to change and the paths that led him to such a terrifying state.

Furthermore, it required analyzing, identifying, dispelling and clarifying such matters and then finally counteracting them with their opposites and suppressing them wisely and accurately. So his companion then questioned him further to discover what had made him change.

Not Using the Negligence of Muslims as an Argument Against the Religion

My brother, what are the reasons for what made you end up as I see? What called you to abandon what you used to practice? If it is right, then you and I can share in it. But, if it is contrary to that, then I know from your intelligence, religiosity, and mannerism that you wouldn't be content with remaining upon what would harm you.

His associate responded by saying:

I won't hide from you that I saw the Muslims in a state that is not pleasing to anyone with high ambition. I saw them in a condition of ignorance, humiliation, and complacency. They were backward. On the other hand, I saw these foreigners had progressed in life. They had mastered fine arts as well as astonishing, awe-inspiring inventions, and superior skilled-industries. I saw that the nations followed them and compliantly lowered their necks. They found themselves controlling the weak nations as they deemed fit, considering them as slaves and workers. I saw within them dignified might that amazed me and sophistication that shocked me.

So I said to myself: This wouldn't be the case if these people weren't those to imitate. If they were not upon the truth while the Muslims were upon falsehood, then they wouldn't be in the condition that I described to you. So I saw that following their way and modeling myself after them is better and best for me in the long run. That is what changed me as you noticed.

Once he had been shown what was hidden, his associate told him:

If this is the cause of what transformed you, then that is not from the valid reasons upon which intelligent, logical persons base their beliefs, morals, deeds, and futures. My friend, listen to me as I analyze this matter that has fooled you and its actual reality:

What you mentioned of the Muslims' backwardness does not come from their religion. Anyone with the slightest degree of insight and vision knows that the religion of Islam invites to rectitude and rectification in both religious and worldly affairs and encourages arming one's self with beneficial sciences and arts. It invites to spiritually strengthening one's self and to physically deterring one's adversaries, to forego their evils and harms. No one ever benefited in a worldly-sense let alone religiously except by way of this religion. Here we have its teachings and instructions calling upon its adherents to hasten to busy themselves with all beneficial means that will exalt and advance them in both a religious and worldly-sense.

Would you use the negligence of the Muslims as an argument against the religion? That is clear oppression.

Isn't it short-sided, whimsical, and fanatical to look at the state of the Muslims' affairs in this era of time when their knowledge and achievements have regressed — an era in which they had lost the establishing values of their religion — without looking at Islam's flourishing and religious state in its foremost days when they were establishing this religion. They strove to take all means which the religion encourages. Thus, their morals and feats advanced to a degree that remains unparalleled by anyone since the past and will continue to be so into the distant future. The entire world from east to west followed them and the most stalwart nations submitted to them. That was because of their true religion and due to the justice, wisdom, mercy and beautiful qualities they possessed.

Doesn't the Muslims' weakness in these times require those of them endowed with vision and courage to multiply their effort, energy, and greatest struggle so as to establish everything in their capacity to reach lofty heights, thereby rescuing themselves from the cavernous abyss into which they have plummeted? Isn't this from the most compelling of duties and binding of requirements in such a circumstance? During the state when the Muslims have power and a multitude of participants this struggle has tremendous merit that surpasses all acts of worship, so how much more is that the case when they're in the situation that you described? The merits and fruits of the struggle are beyond description.

So in this state of affairs, the struggle is two-fold: First: striving to correct the Muslims, awaken their ambitions, excite their determination, to educate them with beneficial studies and refine them with finer morals. That is the more difficult yet most beneficial and superior of these two types. Secondly: striving to curb their adversaries and equip ourselves with every verbal, practical, political, internal and external apparatus to repel them and be spared from their evil.

At a time when the affair has become as I described, and while the position has become so dire would you do away with your Muslim brothers? Would you lag behind with the cowards and opposers? So how could you go beyond that to join those warring against us? I implore you by Allah, my brother, not to be less than those about whom it was said: "Come and fight in Allah's path or at least defend yourselves!" Meaning contend for the sake of your religion or at least provide defense for your people and nation. Don't be like these hypocrites. I pray that you are granted refuge from such a condition with which no adherent to any religion and none with any courage or dignity should be pleased.

Would you be pleased to participate with your people only when they experience might and strength in morale and personnel, yet disavow them while they are degraded and afflicted? Would you forsake them in a state where they are in dire need of supporters to help them and defend against hostility? Have you seen a people or religion better than yours?!

A 'Civilization' of Outer Beauty and Inner Ruin

The recipient of this advice responded:

The situation is just as I mentioned. My ego aspires toward these people who have mastered the arts and industries and have progressed in life.

His associate responded in turn, debating with him:

You've rejected a straight religion that is firmly principled and unquestionably proven. It invites to every good and encourages all happiness and success. It tells its practitioners to rush toward every rectitude and rectification and every goodness and prosperity and to take every path leading you to worldly and everlasting happiness.

It is a religion built upon a genuinely advanced civilization that is erected upon justice and monotheism, based on mercy, wisdom, knowledge, compassion, and rendering rights to others, whether they be of a compulsory or a recommended nature. It is free of oppression, pomp and degenerate immorality. Its expansive shade, far-reaching kindness, all-inclusive goodness, and total brightness

extends over the earth from its eastern to its western
lands. That is admitted by both those who accept it
and those who disagree with it while remaining
objective.

Would you abandon it because you crave after
civilizations and societies erected upon disbelief and
atheism, built upon greed, pompousness, cruelty,
and oppression of people — that which is void of
the spirit of faith and its mercifulness, absent of the
light of knowledge and wisdom. It is a culture
whose exterior is beautified and decorated while
being internally destroyed. You imagine it to
animate the world while in fact it ultimately destroys
and annihilates it. Don't you see its ill-effects in
these times and what it produces of an assortment
of evils and misery and what they have reaped for
humankind of destruction, obliteration, and
annihilation?

Since Allah created this creation, have they ever
heard of anything comparable or equivalent to
these human massacres that this recent course of
'civilization' has reaped? Could their societies and
civilizations spare them from Allah's punishment in
any way whatsoever once the order of your Lord

came to pass? Instead, it only increased them in ruin!

So don't be fooled by what you see of enamored appearances, misleading slogans, and overreaching claims, but instead look at the internal characteristics of matters and their realities and don't be tricked by their appearances. Reflect over the horrible results and blameworthy fruits entailed and whether that has brought them happiness in this world, which is the only life for which they even hope. On the other hand, don't you see them moving from one evil to a multitude of them, never experiencing stability at any time except that soon after that they are instigated to terrifying atrocities and enormous massacres?

Whenever power, civilization, society and every sort of material wealth is devoid of true faith, then this will be its nature, its fruits, and its misery. That is because it doesn't have beneficial fundamentals and principles or suitable aims and objectives.

Grant for the sake of argument that they are made to enjoy life and led slowly but surely to their demises through being granted honor, leadership, and some semblance of power and worldly life: If you were to join them and give them your loyalty, would they let you share it with them? Would they make you like one of their own? By Allah, they absolutely would not! Even if they were pleased with you, they still would not make you equivalent to even one of their disgraced servants.

The evidence of that is that you toil hard for them, serving them night and day. You speak, argue and dispute on their behalf and still, they don't raise you as an equal to even the least of their people and those of their race. My brother, I implore you by Allah concerning your religion, dignity, morality, and etiquette. I reiterate, beseeching you by Allah regarding the rest of your life. By Allah, joining these people is destruction.

Good Companionship & the Danger of Being Distant from It

The recipient of this advice responded:

"What you said is true, but I have educated friends and cultured associates who have adopted this as their way and opinion. I have solidified an agreement with them to abide by agnosticism and belittlement of those who adhere to the religion of the Lord of humankind. We have mutually experienced a substantial amount of pleasures and have permissively allowed whatever our egos suggest of a slew of passions. How could I then shun and boycott these respected people to whom I have become so intimately attached? Now I'm torn by two voices: One calling me to the truth after the way has become obvious, and the proof made clear; the other is my ego and my attachment to these associates, which, in every way, goes against the truth. What is the way to bring me calmness and heal me? How do I get solace in this scenario?"

His advisor said:

Don't you know that from man's most binding duties and greatest virtues is that he follows the apparent truth and abandons whatever falsehood he is engaged in, especially when he is inwardly torn and tempted by selfish worldly ambitions? Don't you know that if someone who once was guided then falls into destructive behavior, he will search after the means to ensure his salvation? Don't you know is from Allah's blessings that Allah's destines for a person to have sincere advisors who direct him toward goodness, order him with righteousness, forbid him from evil and work toward his happiness and success?

Furthermore, from the completion of this blessing is being inspired to cooperating with them, not imitating those whom Allah said about them: "You do not love those who sincerely advise." It is possible that when a person experiences a brief taste of the way of those who have deviated and witnesses what they are involved in of deviance and misguidance, only to then return to the truth so dear to his heart, that it has a more impactful effect and a greater benefit.   So come back to the truth genuinely and be confident of Allah's promise. Verily Allah doesn't break His promise.

The recipient of this advice responded:

It isn't unknown to you that falsehood doesn't easily depart once it penetrates and gains control over the heart. I want you to thoroughly expound on the false nature of what the atheists believe. Indeed, they establish a multitude of doubts to promote their statements so that those without vision are deluded.

His advisor said:

Know that the truth and falsehood are at odds with each other, and that good and evil contradict each other. By knowing either of a set of opposites, the attractiveness or hideousness of the other becomes obvious. So let me inform you in a broad, subtle manner about this.

Whenever you wish to contrast or compare things that are unmistakably different, then look at the foundations and principles upon which they are based and constructed, and then look at their effects, their end-results and the variations of fruits yielded by them. Look at their evidence and proofs by which they are positively affirmed, and then look at what they consist of and contain of rectitude and benefits, or of evils and harms. So once you have looked at these matters with correct understanding and keen intellect, then the issue will become immediately visible to you.

Once you've recognized these foundational matters, then this is the true religion called to by the Messenger Prophets in general and the finality and leader of them, Muhammad, ﷺ in particular. It is built and founded upon monotheism and recognizing Allah alone as a deity worthy of worship without any partner whatsoever deserving a share of what is rightfully His such as love, fear, hope, sincerity, submission, humility for His Lordship, and compliance by servitude.

All logical, natural, and instinctual evidence proves the veracity of this fundamental which is the greatest of them all. All revealed religion proves it and all of the Prophets, the Messengers, and their followers accepted it — those people of strong knowledge, keen intellect, and dignified morality. All agree that Allah alone is uniquely singled out with Oneness and that every Attribute of Perfection is His, making Him describable with nothing less than the height of Majesty, Magnificence, Greatness, and Beauty. They agree that He is the Creator, Sustainer, and Disposer of all affairs. He is free of all imperfection and resemblance to His creation. None but He deserve worship, praise, glorification, and gratitude. The Islamic religion is based on this fundamental and stands upright upon it.

As for what the atheists are upon, then it undoubtedly contradicts this fundamental to the utmost. For verily it is based upon the immediate denial of the Creator, far less than recognizing His Perfection or undertaking the most compelling of obligations which is worshipping Him alone without counterparts. The advocates of this ideology are the worst of people in their obstinance and denial of the most obvious and clear of affairs. What could a person ever admit who denies Allah?

These are the furthest people from worshipping Allah and from turning to Him in devotion. They are the most improbable to ever incorporate commendable character as is called for by all revealed religion and readily admissible to sound intellects. So long as their hearts are missing monotheism, belief in Allah, and its positive effects, then such people would be the most ignorant, most visionless and most clueless of people about the fundamentals and secondary tenets of the Islamic religion. Despite that, you find them writing, speaking and claiming for themselves to have reached a degree of certainty, knowledge, and education unparalleled by the most senior of Islamic religious academics.

At the same time, you would see them inept, not even having reached the degree of the least student of Islamic knowledge when requested to discuss a single fundamental from the tremendous fundamentals of the religion that none could possibly be ignorant of, or to discuss a single ruling pertaining worship, interpersonal transactions or the laws of marriage.

So how could a logical person - let alone a believer - trust their statements about the religion? Their statements about the fundamentals of the religion are worthless from inception. If you analyzed the gist of what their figureheads are upon, you'd see that they've busied themselves with the slightest degree of Arabic studies and have repetitively read papers conforming to their ideology. They've trained themselves to discuss whatever is from the general approach found in these vile, worthless papers. Thus they and their followers suppose these people to be brimming with information and knowledge, while ultimately, the extent of what they reached of religious knowledge is just this.

As for moral character, don't even ask about the morality of someone who doesn't believe in Allah and the last day and who does not have authentic beliefs. For undoubtedly, morality traits are the results of either valid or invalid beliefs. The extent of what they possess is mere flattery in word and deed alongside disingenuous humility to other people. Alongside this debased servility, you find them having a great deal of self-astonishment, arrogance, contempt for others and an aversion to socializing with those who they demean. They are the lowliest of Allah's creation while simultaneously being the most arrogant and pompous.

Beyond that, they employ primping and aesthetics in clothing, furnishing, and decoration to promote what they dub being cultured, devoting a great deal of their time to that while their hearts are void of guidance and beautiful morality. What can inauthentic outer beauty avail against true beauty? Were you to observe their aspirations and goals you would find that they have repulsive aims, degenerate goals, and selfish ambitions.

If you analyze their situations, you would see that when they socialize, you imagine them to be united friends but when they separate they are enemies. "You suppose that they are together, but their hearts are disunited. That is because they are a people with no intelligence."

As you know full well, what I described to you of their circumstances is just a little of much. So how could you ever be pleased with these people being your intimates and friends, being pleased by their pleasure, displeased by their displeasure, and giving them priority over what is really for your advantage and eternal happiness?

Look at their traits and investigate in fairness. Compare between them and the qualities of righteous, good people whose hearts are full of loving Allah and devotion to Him, believing and sincerely working for His sake. Their tongues flow with His remembrance and praise. Their bodies are preoccupied with every means of drawing near to Allah and what pleases Him, and bringing them closer to His reward while being of a benefit to others. They are the most brave-hearted and truthful people. They are the purest of them in moral character and deed. They are the closest to every good and farthest from every evil. They spare people from harm, sacrifice for their benefit and are patient with their wrongs.

Faced with such unique nobility could you then give precedence to people whose hearts brim with doubt and hypocrisy that spills out onto to their exterior, resulting in immorality. They stand up hypocritically, for appearances, and sit in a state of self-flattery, self-astonishment, and arrogance. They have traits of harshness, pretentiousness, and greed. Their defining attribute is disingenuousness, showiness, and servility. They withhold goodness from all people while incorporating every trait of wickedness. In their studies, they comply with every renegade and follow every disgusting lowlife in character.

The Path to Happiness in this World & the Next

The recipient of this advice responded:

"By Allah, you haven't transgressed an atom's weight in describing them. However, I want you to direct me toward the method that gathers between worldly happiness and everlasting happiness for me. People raised with and influenced by the traits of these people aren't going to leave off what they've become accustomed to without strong persuasion. There must be some motivation and longing that attracts them or some deterrent and fear to discourage them."

His companion advised him:

By Allah, you have already found in this religion what you are searching after. By Allah, everything you want and desire exists within it. Indeed it is the religion that gathers between happiness in this world and the hereafter. It contains the pleasures of the heart, soul, and body. You won't miss out on any sound desire of the soul or any happiness except that it will facilitate it for you. It contains what the soul desires and that which pleases the eye.

Let me elaborate for you:

Know that the fundamentals of searched after pleasure are: Firstly, the repose, calmness, tranquility, happiness, and delight of the heart along with the removal of its worry and anguish. Secondly: A person's contentment and tranquility with what they have of physical wants. Thirdly: Using that as a way to bring happiness and gratification. Whoever is granted these three affairs and uses them appropriately will consequently reach everything for which anyone could ever hope. For indeed, all pleasure traces back to what we mentioned.

As for the delights of the heart, its experiencing of joy, and the removal of its anxiety, then the entire foundation of that happens comes about by having complete faith in what Allah invited His worshippers to believe about Him. That occurs by way of uniquely singling Him out as having every Perfect Attribute, occupying the heart with reverence, honor, worship, servitude, and devotion for Him, being sincere to Him inwardly and outwardly, and working for the sake of His Most High Face. That entails all that results from that including genuineness toward Allah's servants, loving good for them, sacrificing within one's capacity in doing what can benefit them and showing kindness toward them. It also entails frequent remembrance of Allah, seeking forgiveness and repenting. Upon being granted these matters, one's heart will attain guidance, mercy, light, and happiness, as well as the removal of unsettledness, worry, and anguish. That will occur to such an extent that it will serve as just a small example of the bliss of the hereafter.

Those suited to experience such a blessed state do not envy the lords and kings of this world because of their pleasure and rulership. Instead, they view what they themselves been granted of these affairs to far surpass what those people have received many times over. This bliss of the heart isn't positively known by anyone until they taste and experience it. For indeed it is as has been said: whoever encounters the delight of such people's bliss unmistakably recognizes it. And doesn't know of it until tomorrow (i.e., the hereafter) would exchange their soul for it! That is just an indication of this bliss of the heart which is the foundation of all happiness.

As for the second matter, then indeed Allah has granted His servants strength and has further given them what comes from that of wealth, family, children, property, etc. People fit into two categories concerning such things. There are some people for whom these favors are a trial and a curse, and other for whom they are enjoyment, goodness, and a gift.

Those who adhere to the true religion react and respond to these favors by thanking Allah and using such things to aid them in obeying the Bestower of all blessings. They know that such things are the most excellent means they have to reach Allah's good pleasure, goodness, and reward — so long as they use them for what for what they were designed and created. On account of such blessings they pleased with Allah in every way. For indeed they know that this is from Allah who has total wisdom in all that He decrees and ordains. He has vast mercy in all that He controls and has endless grace in all that He grants. He is more merciful to them than all people combined. In as much as that they know with certainty that this wholly emanates from the possessor of such greatness, they are satisfied with whatever He gives them, no matter however little or much that may be.

Their hearts are tranquil as opposed to impatiently longing for or expecting what is not destined for them. Once a person has tranquility, contentment, and satisfaction with Allah for what He has granted, they will enjoy the good life. Once you have comprehended this trait of theirs, then you will realize that the pure bliss of this world is the bliss of being satisfied with Allah's provision and that of the heart's tranquility by remembering and obeying Allah. Even if one had nothing but the slightest amount of these matters, namely, strength, health, family, children, etc., then they would be in a state of relief and happiness from two perspectives. They would have an aspect of self-contentment without their soul impatiently being anxious and expecting things that will not happen. Also, they have the perspective of hoping for Allah's immediate and eventual reward for this worship of the heart which surpasses a great deal of physical worship.

In doing so, they worship Allah by recognizing and being pleased with His blessings, hoping that He maintains and completes them, thereby making them a means to attain other favors and a path to everlasting happiness. Undoubtedly, these states of the heart are from the most meritorious acts of obedience and the most distinguished means of nearness.

Isn't there a great difference between the happiness of this person's heart who is engaged in (this type of) worship that is considered the spirit of the religion, having achieved the good life — as compared to the state of another who reacts to these favors with forgetfulness and not admitting the Grace of He who gave him these things, such that it causes him misery from anxiety and stress? He finds that he remains displeased after achieving some selfish goal while still anxiously desiring more. He goes from one state of unease to another because his heart has an extreme attachment to its physical wants. Whenever things turn out contrary to what he wants and expects, he becomes severely agitated. This person is always in a state of continuous aggravation because his physical wants are of such great variety. Although he achieves one thing, he misses out on others. Somethings may cause him limited happiness in some ways while causing sadness in others. His clarity of mind is mixed with agitation while his delight is tainted by sorrow. Where is the good life for this person? The good life is only experienced by those who possess vision and keen intellect, reacting to things with acceptance, satisfaction, and contentment.

As for the third matter, then it is the proper perspective of how to make use of these blessings. An adherent to the true religion utilizes these things in a manner of gratitude to Allah for His favors, being happy with his Grace. By using them, he intends to strengthen himself to worship and obey Allah, which is his reason for existence. He knows that so long as he spends on himself, his family and children, and those near to him, that his spending has reached its proper recipient and has had its proper effect. Spending a lot in such a way doesn't burden him because he says with full conviction: This is the best of recommended deeds that I could do. That is the greatest thing for which I hope that Allah repays me, in as much as that He, who is Generous and Loyal to His word, said:

﴿ وَمَا أَنفَقْتُم مِّن شَيْءٍ فَهُوَ يُخْلِفُهُ ۖ وَهُوَ خَيْرُ الرَّازِقِينَ ﴾

"Whatsoever you spend then He will replace it, and he is the best of providers."[2]

Such a person continually focuses on effortfully earning and spending in a variety of ways, being

---

[2] Sabʾa 34: 39.

well aware of the Prophet's saying: "You never spend anything seeking thereby Allah's face except that you're rewarded thereupon, even for what you place in the mouth of your wife."

Whoever fits this description will experience untainted, true pleasure from his worldly enjoyments alongside Allah's immediate and eventual reward that he hopes to attain. Whoever matches this description will find it easy to acquire it legally and use it correctly. His affairs will become very easy. As for someone using these blessings greedily and heedlessly, then he tends to be unmindful of continually recognizing Allah's bounty and favors. He doesn't rejoice because these blessings are from Allah's Grace. Instead, he only celebrates because it agrees with some selfish aim. He doesn't intend by doing so to utilize it to aid him in Allah's obedience. He does not intend to work toward a heavenly reward by acquiring it and dispensing it to its proper recipients.

Agitation and sadness will hunt after a person who meets this description. Whenever he misses out on some physical passions, then he becomes sad. No matter what happens this person will be disheartened if things weren't what he had in mind.

He gets sad even if his child or a relative expects mandatory or recommended financial support or clothing, not   spending it except begrudgingly. When he does spend, then a portion of happiness leaves his heart at the same time because he loves the continuance of his wealth and becomes troubled by its reduction. He doesn't have a level of longing for heavenly reward that could ease the matter for him.   This is the scenario when he isn't even necessarily greedy. If, beyond that, he is miserly and innately greedy then living with his family, children and relatives will be a life of misery, torment, frequent bitterness, and sadness. He doesn't possess a level of faith that eases for him to spend nor does he have a generous personality that is uninhibited from reaching nobility.   How awful is his ever-present and continuous inner-torment.   Where is this person compared to the one who attained the fullness of the good life?

All of this happens by taking these three things into consideration that represent the basis of all delight in the estimation of the intelligent.   It has become clear that the possessor of authentic faith is the one who successfully acquires true delight and is free of all that unsettles him.

Contrasting the Believer's State During Calamity to that of an Unbeliever

If we were to take a look at those personal emergencies that none could avoid, then they are minor and major tragedies people undergo such as different sorts of illness, the death of loved ones, the loss and decrease of wealth, hard time's falling upon one's loved ones, and any decline in what is preferable. You see that the true believer reacts with strength, patience and seeking reward. He is anticipant of heavenly reward, knowing that it is the decree of the All-Mighty, All-Knowing and that these are divine preordainments emanating from the Most Merciful Lord. Therefore the matter is lessened, and its effect is lightened.

When he thinks about the grueling pains that it contains, then he contrasts that with what it entails of the removal of sins, the multiplication of good deeds, the elevation of status and the development of noble character traits, inner-strength, and courage.

When his body and wealth is exhausted, he views it as a benefit to his heart and soul. For indeed the hearts' rectitude occurs by thanking Allah for his many blessings and having patience over His tests, awaiting deliverance from Allah when disasters strike while taking recourse to Allah at the onset of every upsetting and unsettling affair. The least case scenario with such a believer is that he will contrast between what is preferable and what is not, and between delight and sorrow. The situation of the most excellent of believers reaches such an extent that their happiness and joy when calamities strike are more than what is normally experienced (by others) of sadness and unsettledness in the soul.

Compare this scenario to that of a person who experiences these tragedies that no person can avoid with an upset, terrified heart that feels humiliated by what it encounters of difficulties and hardships. Sorrow continually returns to his heart and soul, only making the calamity worse on his heart than it is on his body, not having patience and expectation of heavenly reward to lighten his sorrows or the necessary faith to lessen his despair. Calamities strike him, not finding him able to reduce their impact, and so they coursed through his heart, soul, body and his entire situation. His heart is full of worry, sorrow, and pain. Fear of the past and future fills his soul, causing his mind to dissolve and shatter.

His reliance upon Allah was at the depths of weakness until his heart attached itself to people, expecting their benefit. How terrible these worldly calamities prove to be when they become compounded by religious and moral calamity, until seeming to be like unscalable mountains?

By Allah, if they knew what was involved, the people of calamity and affliction would rush to faith, being spirited, comforted and enjoying living life no matter how dire the situation whose anguish required relief. They will never experience that except within genuine, true faith and that which invites a person to it.

The Condition of the Believer in Dealing with People as Compared to that of an Unbeliever

Also, from that which is pertinent to joyous, blissful living and to living with sorrow and grief is one's treatment of people according to their individual levels. Whoever treats them according to what the religion calls for will find relief, and whoever deals with them as their selfish impulses call for will unavoidably have an upsetting tragedy-filled life.

To elaborate, then people are of three types: superiors, subordinates, and peers. As for one who has authority in government or wealth, having aides and assistants, then at any given time, he encounters situations related to both his treatment of them and their good or ill-treatment of him — predicated on his agreeability or disagreeability with them. So long as he behaves according to the religion in such situations, he'll find relief and reward from Allah. While seeking Allah's reward, he is to observe justice, goodwill, benevolence and is to repay their poor treatment with pardoning and gratitude for their excellent work. Likewise, while recalling what he is engaged in of good behavior, he'll find inner peace and his chest will find comfort.

Where is this in comparison to a leader with a nonchalant attitude about oppressing people as far as their lives, property, and honor is concerned. He doesn't care about abiding by the channels of justice and objectivity nor does he possess patience over any harm he experiences from his subordinates. He suffers constant discomfort in dealing with his subordinates, and the hearts of his dependents are full of disdain and hatred of him. They wait for him to fail and look for vulnerable opportunities. They would even aid their worst enemies against him if he committed the smallest error. He can find no comfort with them concerning his life or his worldly privileges, not knowing when disaster may strike, morning and evening. That, in summary, is the leader's situation.

As for the subordinate's situation, then one is to obey the religion regarding his societal function while also complying with his ruler, master, or parent, treating them according to what religious etiquette and pleasing character calls for. So long as he does so while obeying Allah and His Messenger, he'd find relief while being a relief for others, and will find his superiors good spirited. He will be safe of any penalty and will be hopeful of goodness, benevolence, and love in return. Were he to transgress his bounds, disobey his superior and turn for the worse, then he'd expect all sort of harm. In turn he would tread in dread, trembling and experiencing utter instability, finding no relief.

As for the situation concerning an equal and peer, then they are indeed the vast majority of the people with whom you interact. So long as you treat them with upright character, then your soul will be at peace and worries will vanish from you because you would earn their love and remove their animosity along with expecting Allah's tremendous reward for such treatment — which constitutes one of the most superior acts of worship. For surely, by his exemplary character, the worshipper reaches the degree of a person who perpetually fasts (by day) and prays by night. Furthermore, having good character has a specificity regarding the happiness of the soul. None know this except those who experience it. Where is such a person in contrast to another who treats people with the worst character? His good is withheld while his evil is not spared from others. He doesn't have the slightest degree of patience for what he encounters of troubles. The life of such a person is dismal, regularly feeling worried and remorseful. He is continually perturbed and fearful of some impending doom.

As for one's treatment of immediate family, children, and relatives, then he makes sure to attend to necessary rights and duties perfectly without deficiency or being irritable. If he interacts with them as Allah and His Messenger ﷺ have commanded while being hopeful of his Lord's reward and good pleasure, then he will live a pleasant life with them. Whoever acts aggravated and ill-mannered toward those that are younger or older than them will leave their home angry and enter upon their family annoyed and weary. What kind of life would a person have in such a state? What could he ever hope for in as much as that he ruined that which causes his happiness and joy?

As for one's treatment of those with who they do business, then if he treats them with goodwill and genuineness while being easy going when selling, buying, and settling debts, then he will obtain divine mercy. He will also succeed in attaining honor and high esteem. He will earn the love of those he does business with and will retain their business. It is no secret that this leads to an enjoyable life and the cheerfulness of such a person. The opposite indicates a poor state, a loss of dignity, and a depressed life.

The distinguishing factor between these two men is the religion. The religiously devoted person is outgoing in personality and tranquil in his heart. It has now become abundantly clear to you that happiness and genuine pleasure of every type result from this religion.

The Pleasure of Holding Fast to the Religion

The religion comprises of two types of things:

Firstly: Actions, circumstances and moral qualities that are related to the religion and the world simultaneously. As we mentioned, there's no way to secure a good life without the religion.

Secondly: Sciences and useful information, namely, the scholastic sciences of the religion and whatever aids and contributes to their implementation. Preoccupation with this if from the most illustrious acts of worship and acquiring its fruits is from the most perfect of pleasures. Nothing of worldly pleasures resemble it. Consider this by looking at the state of those interested in knowledge. You'll find that most of their time is devoted to acquiring knowledge. A long time will pass and such a person will be still engrossed while wishing for more time. This is the essence of delight. A person who is immersed in it will find a lengthy stretch of time to feel short while a person uncomfortable with it will feel that a short period seems long.

The partaker in knowledge is benefitting at all times from different aspects of knowledge whereby his faith increases and his character is perfected. A person who turns the pages of beneficial books will perpetually subject his mind to the intellects, information and commendable circumstances of the earlier and later generations. Certainly the intelligent person can likewise take heed from the opposite scenario. How many stories do you encounter inside of these books that instill additional intelligence within you? This comforts you during hardship because you realize what the virtuous people have endured and how they reacted by being content and submitting and how they ultimately profited by being rewarded by the All Knowing, All Wise. Therefore, knowledge acquaints you with the ways by which you reach your goals and repels away from you all that is disliked and harmful.

Two Types of Intelligence

There are two types of intelligence. Natural intelligence which comes from having a strong mind about both worldly and religious matters. This is placed in a person by Allah. The other is earned intelligence. When this is combined with natural intelligence it increases a person's determination and insight. It is then similar to natural intelligence and thrives through personal development until a person reaches firmness.

That being the case, natural intelligence has two elemental sources for development. One source is by congregating with the intelligent and benefitting from their minds and experience. Sometimes this is done by taking their example and sometimes this happens by mutual consultation and questioning them. How great is the progress that a man makes by doing this and as a result he advances to the heights of success? For this reason a person's reclusiveness away from other people makes him miss out on much good and splendid benefit. Along with that, reclusiveness causes him to imagine and have ill-suspicion about people, as well as self astonishment which demonstrates one's personal shortcomings. Perhaps it may also harm the body.

Interacting with people opens up doors of good, and it comforts you and strengthens the heart. Having a weak heart is harmful to the mind, religion, character and health.

Thus it is befitting to deal with people according to their situations just as the Prophet used good character with the young and old. Allah said:

﴿ خُذِ الْعَفْوَ وَأْمُرْ بِالْعُرْفِ وَأَعْرِضْ عَنِ الْجَاهِلِينَ ﴾

"Take what is given freely, enjoin what is good, and turn away from the ignorant."[3]

Meaning: Accept what comes natural of people's characteristics and leave alone that which comes forcibly. When sitting with worldly people such a person displays etiquette and dignity. He sits respectably with elders. He is outgoing with his brothers and companions. He is merciful and humble toward the poor. He treats the people of knowledge and religion as is befitting for their virtuous status. You see someone with such character elated in spirit and experiencing a good life.

---

[3] Al 'Arāf: 199.

The second source of acquirable intelligence is preoccupation with beneficial knowledge. Each issue (of knowledge) will bring you benefit by formulating a new view and stronger reasoning. A person preoccupied with knowledge perpetually advances in knowledge, intelligence and etiquette. Knowledge acquaints you with Allah and the path leading to Him. It acquaints you with how to employ acceptable manners in such a way that it draws you nearer to Allah while intended as worship. Knowledge assumes the status of leadership and wealth — whoever reaches knowledge has reached everything, whereas whoever misses out on knowledge misses out on everything. This is exclusive to beneficial knowledge. On the other hand, books of superstition and shamelessness destroy morality while corrupting hearts and minds by encouraging them to take evil people as role models, having an effect on faith and the heart equivalent to that of fire on straw.

The recipient of the advice responded:

I swear by Allah, how I felt at the beginning of discussing this subject is now resolved and the falsehood vanished during your explanation. The fact that you sat and advised me in such a beneficial way is worth more to me than the world and everything in it, my brother. So I praise Allah first that He appointed you for me and then I thank you immensely that you loyally fulfilled the right of friendship and didn't do what some intellectuals do by cutting off the rope of affection as soon as they see something displeasing and thus aid Satan against that person. By doing so, the evil effecting them is only increased and their mutual willingness for understanding is lost. For a surety, I won't forget this beautiful kindness of yours. You saw me stumbling about confused, deluded and impressed with my own opinion, so you showed me with my own eyes what I am involved in. You stopped me with your wisdom so I could realize the destruction I'd fallen into. Now I seek Allah's forgiveness from what preceded and repent to Him. I ask Him to aid me in pursuing His pleasure. I turn fearfully to Him so that He might allow me to conclude my deeds upon righteousness. I praise Allah, first and last, outwardly and inwardly. Indeed He is the guardian of blessing, protecter from harm and He is abundant in generosity and honoring.

Appendix 1: Islamic Culture versus Modern Culture

Severe insistence on 'modern culture' is a matter by which deviant individuals promote their falsehood, claiming that moral character cannot be refined or balanced without it. They extensively praise it and its advocates, while criticizing and mocking those lacking such 'culture.' They explain it in different, deviant ways, with each one of them saying what springs to their mind. If knowledge is chaotic with morality following suit, then this is predictive of how such people will be overall. They will not agree in their theories, work, and morals.

We are unable to fully elaborate on precisely what they say about this misguided sort of culture. However, people of knowledge, keen mindedness, and advanced intellect know that it amounts to a collapse of moral character and a departure away from actual spiritual matters. It stands for vanity, conceitedness, and pride. This is the greatest sickness with which a person can be afflicted.

The only valid culturing and beneficial refinement are, in fact, what the Islamic religion has procured; for assuredly, it is impossible for the self's culturing and for the development of virtue to happen by way of purely material secular sciences and what they produce. The observable world is the most significant witness to that. Despite the evolution and depth of science, it is utterly incapable of rectifying moral character and acquiring virtue, just as it is incapable of lifting people out of vice. The only thing to dependably undertake this rectification, to assume this genuine refinement, and to direct human thought toward true knowledge, action, goodness, guidance, and rectitude while discouraging it from every evil is what the Islamic religion has brought. It is a rectification for both the exterior and interior, for beliefs, moral character, and actions; it encourages every virtue while discouraging every vice.

The spirit of what the Islamic religion invites to is the belief in the unseen. It consists of belief in Allah the Magnificent and all that He has of Beautiful Names, perfect, lofty Attributes, praiseworthy actions, and perfect control; it also consists of belief in immediate and eventual recompense for righteous and evil deeds, respectively — the details of which are unknowable except through the Messengers. This plants within the heart the desire to perform virtuous acts and good deeds, and a competitiveness to attain the station of excellence in worshipping Allah while imparting goodness to the creation. It also implants a hatred of evil and vice, and it is that which has a tremendous effect in rectifying individuals and society. Allah, describing the believers, said:

﴿ وَلَكِنَّ اللَّهَ حَبَّبَ إِلَيْكُمُ الْإِيمَانَ وَزَيَّنَهُ فِي قُلُوبِكُمْ وَكَرَّهَ إِلَيْكُمُ الْكُفْرَ وَالْفُسُوقَ وَالْعِصْيَانَ ۚ أُولَٰئِكَ هُمُ الرَّاشِدُونَ ﴾

"However Allah has endeared faith to you and beautified it in your hearts while causing you to abhor disbelief, sinfulness, and disobedience. Such persons are the rightly guided ones. It is a favor from Allah and a blessing, and Allah is All-Knowing, All-Wise."[4]

So it directs the entirety of thought, intention, and action toward every goodness while discouraging it from everything harmful; it orders it with justice, imparting kindness to others, and giving to kith and kin—while forbidding lewdness, evil, and oppression against people as regards life, property, reputation, and rights. As for purely material science, then it is dry and does not motivate its learners to be honorable, or discourage them from wickedness and evil. Instead, their inner-

---

[4] Al Ḥujurāt 49: 7

selves become purely mechanical—viler than the selves of predatory animals, exclusively working toward their selfish pursuits, whatever those may be.

How significant is the difference between a heart full of belief in Allah, desire for His reward and good-pleasure and fear of His displeasure and punishment, while its moral character is the best and most perfect? This faith and all that results from it has an effect on his self-direction, his guidance of others, and his entire endeavor. So, therefore, his actions are righteous; he was sincere to Allah, fulfilling the rights of His slaves such that he zealously safeguarded his covenants and trusts, being respectful of everyone's rights and all interpersonal dealings. Every person feels at peace about his reliability, his trustworthiness, and his establishment of the rights binding upon him. How significant is the difference between this person and someone who is the complete opposite?

The latter does not have an aorta of faith in his heart, does not desire goodness or fear evil, nor does he abide by covenants and trusts. All who know him and are intimately acquainted with him are not confident about his reliability and trustworthiness; he does not have a fear of Allah to deter him from forbidden matters and treachery. The moral character of such a person has plummeted to the lowest of depths; his confidence and ambition are purely focused upon primping his body and hair, and to beautifying his apparel, appearance, and speech. Behind that facade there is nothing besides shame and ruin owing to what he is insistent upon of traits that corrupt his entire situation and that of those attached to him. Between these two types of people is the distance from the heaven to earth. This enormous difference is traceable to whether a person imparts lifeless 'modern culture' or the culture of the religion whose spirit is mercy, justice, fairness, trustworthiness, and loyalty in fulfilling rights.

Therefore, the most excellent favor by which Allah blesses His servant is inner-vision whereby he sees things as they are. So he knows the truth and enacts it while knowing falsehood and abandoning it. Allah alone is the One that guides. Do not look at a person who identifies as Muslim while casting moral character behind his back, using him as an argument against Islam and the Muslims due to his ill-traits, his stagnancy, and his moral corruption. For assuredly, Islam and true Muslims free themselves from someone in such a state even if he calls himself a Muslim — while really possessing nothing of Islam except for a semblance.

For indeed, the Islamic religion is a religion of loftiness, honor, and true advancement. Its teachings, directives, moral character, and deeds all assume the epitome of precision and structure. It has the maximum degree of guidance to every sort of goodness, correctness, and righteousness for whoever abides by it. Everyone knows what the earliest Muslims occupied of completeness and the establishment of all essential worldly and religious facets. They set the excellent standard for human perfection unrivaled by anything else. Whoever wants to know the beautiful effects of the religion, then let him look at them. As for one who wants to reject and delude others pridefully, then they will have a different outlook than this. Allah's aid alone is sought.[5]

---

[5] Excerpted from the short treatise Usūl al-Dīn. Majmū' Muallafāt al-Sa'dī.

Appendix 2: The Qualities of the Believer & the Fruits of Belief[6]

Allah, in His book, has described the believer as affirming and conceding to all of the religion's beliefs, wanting what Allah loves and is pleased with, acting in accordance to what Allah loves and is pleased with, and abandoning all acts of disobedience. He hastens to repent from anything that he committed of that and his faith has impacted his character, statements, and actions in the most wholesome way.

So He described the believers as believing in the comprehensive fundamentals, namely: belief in Allah, His angels, His scriptures, His messengers, the Last Day, and in predestination of what is good and bad; they believe in all that was brought by every Messenger; and they believe in the unseen. He described them as listening and obeying, as well complying outwardly and inwardly. He described them as follows:

﴿ الَّذِينَ إِذَا ذُكِرَ اللَّهُ وَجِلَتْ قُلُوبُهُمْ وَإِذَا تُلِيَتْ عَلَيْهِمْ آيَاتُهُ

---

[6] from the book al Qawā'id al Ḥisān al Muta'alliqah bi Tafsīr al Qurān by 'Abd al-Raḥmān al-Sa'dī.

53

زَادَتْهُمْ إِيمَاناً وَعَلَى رَبِّهِمْ يَتَوَكَّلُونَ * الَّذِينَ يُقِيمُونَ الصَّلاةَ وَمِمَّا رَزَقْنَاهُمْ يُنْفِقُونَ * أُولَئِكَ هُمُ الْمُؤْمِنُونَ حَقّاً ﴾

"[2.] (They are) those who, when Allah is mentioned, feel a fear in their hearts and when His Verses (this Qur'an) are recited unto them, they (i.e. the Verses) increase their Faith; and they put their trust in their Lord (Alone); [3.] Who perform As-Salat (Iqamat-as-Salat) and spend out of that We have provided them. [4.] It is they who are the believers in truth."[7]

He described them as having skin that trembles, eyes that flood with tears, and hearts that soften and find tranquility with Allah's verses and mention. They give what they give with trembling hearts because they are sure to return to their Lord. He described them as observing humble veneration in their general affairs, and as especially adopting it during prayer. They shun idle speech. They attend to purification (of both their wealth and hearts). They preserve their chastity from anything except for their wives and right-hand possessions. They abide by their testimonies and are mindful of their trusts and covenants.

---

[7] Al Anfāl 8: 2-4.

He described them as having perfect certainty without any doubt and as striving with their wealth and lives in Allah's path. He described them as having sincerity for their Lord in all that they give and withhold. He described them as loving the believers; praying for their believing brothers who came before them and come after them; striving diligently to remove hatred from their hearts toward the believers; having allegiance to Allah and the Messenger, and to Allah's believing worshippers. They disassociate from the religion's foes and they command with goodness while forbidding evil. They obey Allah and the Messenger ﷺ in every circumstance.

So Allah gathered within the (believers) true beliefs, total certainty and the perfect practice of regularly turning (to Him). This results in their complying by implementing commandments, abstaining from forbidden matters, and stopping short from exceeding the religion's parameters.

These noble qualities are the description of the absolute believer who is safe from punishment and deserving of reward, who attains every good resulting from faith. For assuredly, Allah, in His book, has designated benefits and fruits related to ēmān that are no fewer than one hundred benefits in number. Each one of them is better than the world and all that it contains.

He has made attainment of His good-pleasure, which surpasses everything, to result from faith. Also, He has also made the following matters to emerge from faith: entrance into paradise; salvation from hell-fire; security from the punishment of the grave, from the difficulties of Judgment Day, and from their affairs falling into disarray. They will have perfect glad-tidings in this life and in the Hereafter, and they will have resoluteness upon faith and obedience in this world, at the time of death. They will have it in the grave by having faith and tawḥīd and through the beneficial correct response (to the questions of the angels). Also, as a result of faith, He has facilitated for them a wholesome life, sustenance, goodness, and ultimate ease in this world. They will be made distant from extreme hardship. They will have repose in their hearts, relaxation of the soul and total satisfaction. They will experience rightness in their overall condition and with their offspring, who will be the coolness of the believer's eye. They will enjoy patience during tribulations and calamities, Allah's removal of their burdens, Allah's defending them against all evils, and triumph against the enemy. They will have an excuse from any accountability due to being forgetful, ignorant, and being mistaken. Allah has removed the previous hardships and shackles (imposed upon earlier nations) and has not made them bear more than they are able. Because of faith, He forgives them of their sins and guides them to repentance.

Therefore faith is the most significant means of nearness to Allah and His mercy, as well as attainment of His reward. It is the most excellent means of forgiveness of sins and for the removal and alleviation of all hardships. In detail, the fruits of faith are many, yet in summary, all of the good in this world and the hereafter result from ēmān, just as all evils result from an absence thereof. And Allah knows best.

Appendix 3: The Perfection & Appeal of Islam

From the most significant mistakes and worst errors is that of Islamic governments, societies, and individuals deriving their various systems and laws from foreign systems despite their being at the height of defect and deficiency. At the same time, they leave off seeking the sources of such things from their religion despite it being complete and perfecting while protecting against evil and corruption.

Nothing seems to remain of Islam except for its name and a trace of it. We call ourselves Muslims, yet we abandon the main components, foundations, and actions of our religion only to go off and glean that from the outsiders. The reason for that is substantial ignorance about the religion, having good thoughts about the outsiders, and witnessing the current defect and weakness of the Muslims in all areas of life, both spiritual and material. As a result of all of that, many faces have turned in interest toward obtaining such things from outsiders, only increasing us in weakness, defect, corruption, and harm in the process.

Otherwise, if we knew with actual knowledge, then we would see that our religion contains advanced concepts, lofty character, just systems, and sound foundations that delight the souls and peak people's interest. We would come to know that all of humankind is in desperate need of taking shelter under its expansive shade that shields against far-reaching evil. So what concept, fundamental, or action that benefits humanity is there that the Islamic religion doesn't endorse? Doesn't it do so in a manner proving that it is capable of facilitating a complete life built upon such principles and foundations? It contains the solution for military and economic problems, as well as all of life's other dilemmas that nations must solve in order to live happily.

Aren't its beliefs the most correct of all beliefs and the most reformative for the hearts, without which the hearts cannot be set right? Is there anything more valid, beneficial, and greater in proof than the sound conviction of belief and certain knowledge of the fact that we have a tremendous Lord whose magnificence and greatness is as such that the greatness of all creation pales in comparison to it? He has the most beautiful Names and the loftiest Divine Attributes. He has power over all things and knowledge of all things, so nothing escapes Him. Nothing in the earth or the heavens is hidden from Him. He is Ever-Merciful such that His Mercy accommodates everything. His Generosity fills the entirety of the world above and below. He is Wise pertaining all that He created and all that He revealed of religion. He has created everything perfectly and has revealed His religion in precise detail. He answers the prayers of those who call upon Him. He grants relief to the desperate. He alleviates the anxiety of those in worry. Whoever trusts in Him, then He will suffice them. Whoever turns to him, seeking His nearness, then He brings that person close and nearer. He shelters whoever seeks His safe-haven. None besides Him can genuinely facilitate goodness and righteousness, and none besides Him alleviate evil and harm. He endears Himself to His creation in every way while guiding them to every path. None depart away from His goodness, honorable treatment, and generosity except for the rebellious and wicked. Can the hearts and souls retain wellness by any other means than conceding that He is their sole Deity and worshipping Him? Who else shares with Allah in any of these matters that are specific to Him?

The same is the case with character. This religion only guides to the best of it. Have you ever seen a perfect quality except that it commands with it? There are no beneficial qualities that it doesn't encourage. There is no good except that it guides to it and there is no evil except that it warns against it. Doesn't it promote truthfulness and justice in word and deed? Doesn't it command with sincerity for Allah in all circumstances? Doesn't it encourage all variety of kindness for every type of creature? Doesn't it command with aiding the oppressed, delivering those in dire straits, and removing harm from those in desperate need? Doesn't it encourage that good character be employed in every situation regardless of how familiar or unfamiliar a person may be, or whether he be a foe or a friend? (Allah) said [what means]:

﴿ ادْفَعْ بِالَّتِي هِيَ أَحْسَنُ فَإِذَا الَّذِي بَيْنَكَ وَبَيْنَهُ عَدَاوَةٌ كَأَنَّهُ وَلِيٌّ حَمِيمٌ ﴾

"Repel [evil] by that [deed] which is better; and thereupon the one whom between you and him is enmity [will become] as though he was a devoted friend."[8]

Doesn't it forbid lying, foulness, and betrayal of

---

[8] Fuṣṣilat 41: 34.

all sorts? Doesn't it encourage careful observance of testimonies and trusts? Doesn't it warn against oppressing people by violation of life, property, and reputation? There is no virtuous characteristic except that it commanded with it and there is no reprehensible trait except that it forbade against it. For that reason, the most significant principle of this religion is that of **safeguarding all that is advantageous while protecting against all evils**.

Furthermore, if we were to look at its approach to life and how it contends with other communities, then we would see that it contains every system relevant to benefit and defense! Doesn't it contain the commandment to pursue sustenance through every beneficial, legal manner of business, skilled industry, agriculture, and every sort of employment? It hasn't banned a single useful means (of wealth) in any way. It has only forbidden harmful transactions, namely, those consisting of oppression, harm, or gambling. Also, from its attractive tenets is that it forbade these exact categories of things whose corruption and harms are clear. Doesn't it contain the command to take precaution against the enemy and to shield ourselves from their abuses by all necessary means? Doesn't it include the order to prepare the means that protect against enemies according to one's respective time, place, and ability?

Doesn't it encourage unity and harmony — the core pillar for cooperative work that produces the greater good in a religious and world sense? Doesn't it forbid what runs counter to that of division? Doesn't it contain an obligation for each person to undertake that which has a definite advantage and apparent benefit, as well as the commandment to conduct mutual consultation about things that are ambiguous? Doesn't it contain guidance toward a variety of methods that accomplish justice and mercy? Doesn't it encourage that implementation of that should be carried out for all of creation?

Doesn't it contain the encouragement to loyally fulfill contracts, treaties, and all major and minor transactions that constitute what is fundamental for the survival of people? Doesn't it include the concept of preventatively seizing hold of the hands of the foolish and criminals in a manner matching their crimes, as well as deterring them by sanctions and punishments that prevent and reduce crime? What matter of benefit exists outside of this religion's directions? Is there any foundation or fundamental containing good and rectitude except that this religion has directed toward it regardless of whether it is of a religious or worldly nature?

To summarize all of that — in this religion Allah has clarified for His servants that He has created them for His worship, which consists of knowing Him and seeking His nearness with all statements, deeds, wealth and beneficial service. He made everything in existence already prepared for them and subject to their use for the purpose of facilitating all that benefits them. He ordered them to obtain these blessings by every available method and means that would enable them to accomplish that, and to utilize such things to help them obey the One who bestowed the blessings.

So is there anyone lower or more oppressive and ignorant than those who turn away from this religion that constitutes the height and extent of all perfection? It is the highest aim of the people of reason and intelligence, yet some go away searching elsewhere after guidance and benefit while claiming to be Muslim?! Their search for another source only increases them in deviance and misguidance.

Whoever exploits what he sees of the condition

of the Muslims, using as his argument the fact that they have fallen far behind in keeping up with the institutions of other nations, then he has committed injustice. For assuredly, the Muslims have not truly established what the religion calls for and have not used it to judge in their religious and worldly matters. They have cast the main components and spirit of their religion aside, and have sufficed to retain the title without its essence, the word without its meaning, and the rough outline without the factual reality! It is mandatory for such people to look at the teachings and instructions of the religion — at its fundamentals and wise purposes, and at what it invites all humanity toward — which entails a wide-array of good for them. For this reason, fair-minded outsiders, despite their beliefs, admit to its completeness and to the fact that there is no way to remove evil from the world except by accepting its teachings, morals, and guidance.

Just as the religion is the real connection between the servants and their Lord — by which they seek His nearness and endearment and by which He showers them with the good of this world and the Hereafter — then indeed it is also the connection of the servants between themselves. Their lives are established through it and their political, economic, and financial problems are solved by it. Every alternative solution contains more harm than benefit and more evil than good. If, for argument's sake, we imagined that other systems could resolve specific issues, then after contemplating that solution you would unmistakably find it connected to the religion. That is because the religion guides to whatever is "most correct" which is a term that includes everything without any exception. Reality itself attests to that.

All of life's energy comes to fruition through the religion, with each person deriving religious and worldly benefit from others. This contrary to what some deluded individuals who are paid to reject the truth claim, saying that it is an opiate holding people back from the benefits of life! By Allah, they have uttered a terrible and audacious lie! Which elements of life has it delayed or stopped? Which has it fallen short of reaching the limit of — in a manner attainable by humankind?

If they are truthful, then let them produce a single example from the religion and not from the misrepresentation shown by the circumstances of some who affiliate with the religion while not abiding by it.[9]

---

[9] Al-Riyāḍ al-Nāḍirah, pp. 127-131. Dar al Minhāj, First Edition (2005).

Notes:

Notes:

ABOUT THE AUTHOR

'Abd al-Raḥmān bin Nāṣir al-Sa'dī رَحِمَهُ ٱللَّهُ (1307-1376 h.) was a famous contemporary scholar who died in the late 1950's. His writings demonstrate his depth of knowledge about Islam as well as an intimate awareness about the world in which he lived and the suitability of Islamic teachings to solve the problems of humankind in all times and places. He is best known for his famous Tafsīr of the Quran. He authored many useful books on Islamic beliefs and law. His writings exist in nearly thirty printed volumes that have undergone multiple editions. May Allah shower him with mercy and reward him with goodness on behalf of the Muslims that have benefited from his legacy of religious knowledge.

Made in the USA
Middletown, DE
20 February 2024

49407170R00040